The Kangaroo

This book has been reviewed
for accuracy by

Merlin D. Tuttle, Ph.D.
Curator of Mammals
Milwaukee Public Museum

Copyright © 1979, Raintree Publishers Limited Partnership

All rights reserved. No part of this book may be reproduced or utilized in any form or by any means, electronic or mechanical, including photocopying, recording, or by any information storage and retrieval system, without permission in writing from the Publisher. Inquiries should be addressed to Raintree Publishers, 310 West Wisconsin Avenue, Milwaukee, Wisconsin 53203.

Library of Congress Number: 79-13660

5 6 7 8 9 0   99 98 97 96 95 94 93 92 91 90 89

Printed in the United States of America.

Library of Congress Cataloging in Publication Data.

Hogan, Paula Z.
 The kangaroo.

 Cover title: The life cycle of the kangaroo.
 SUMMARY: Describes in simple terms the life cycle of kangaroos.
 1. Kangaroos — Juvenile literature. [1. Kangaroos] I. Mayo, Gretchen. II. Title. III. Title: The life cycle of the kangaroo.
QL737.M35H63   599'.2   79-13660
ISBN 0-8172-1504-2 lib. bdg.

The KANGAROO

By Paula Z. Hogan
Illustrations by Gretchen Mayo

RAINTREE CHILDRENS BOOKS
Milwaukee

The Kangaroo

On hot days kangaroos rest under trees. Between short naps they stand up and look around. This way kangaroos are hard to surprise.

After sunset kangaroos begin to feed. They walk on all fours, eating green grass.

Kangaroos live in small groups called mobs. An older male leads each mob. When other males try to take his place, the leader defends himself.

Kangaroos move from place to place, looking for food and water. Many mobs may eat in the same area.

If no rain falls, the grass turns brown. Water holes dry up. Kangaroos die because there isn't enough to eat or drink.

Dingoes are wild dogs that hunt kangaroos. By moving and feeding after dark, kangaroos are harder to find and kill.

A kangaroo thumps its feet on the ground when dingoes are near. In seconds all the kangaroos hop far away.

Kangaroos never run. They hop on their strong back legs. Most animals can't catch the fast kangaroo.

Just before giving birth, the female cleans her pouch. A newborn kangaroo is about the size of a bean. It cannot see and has no hair.

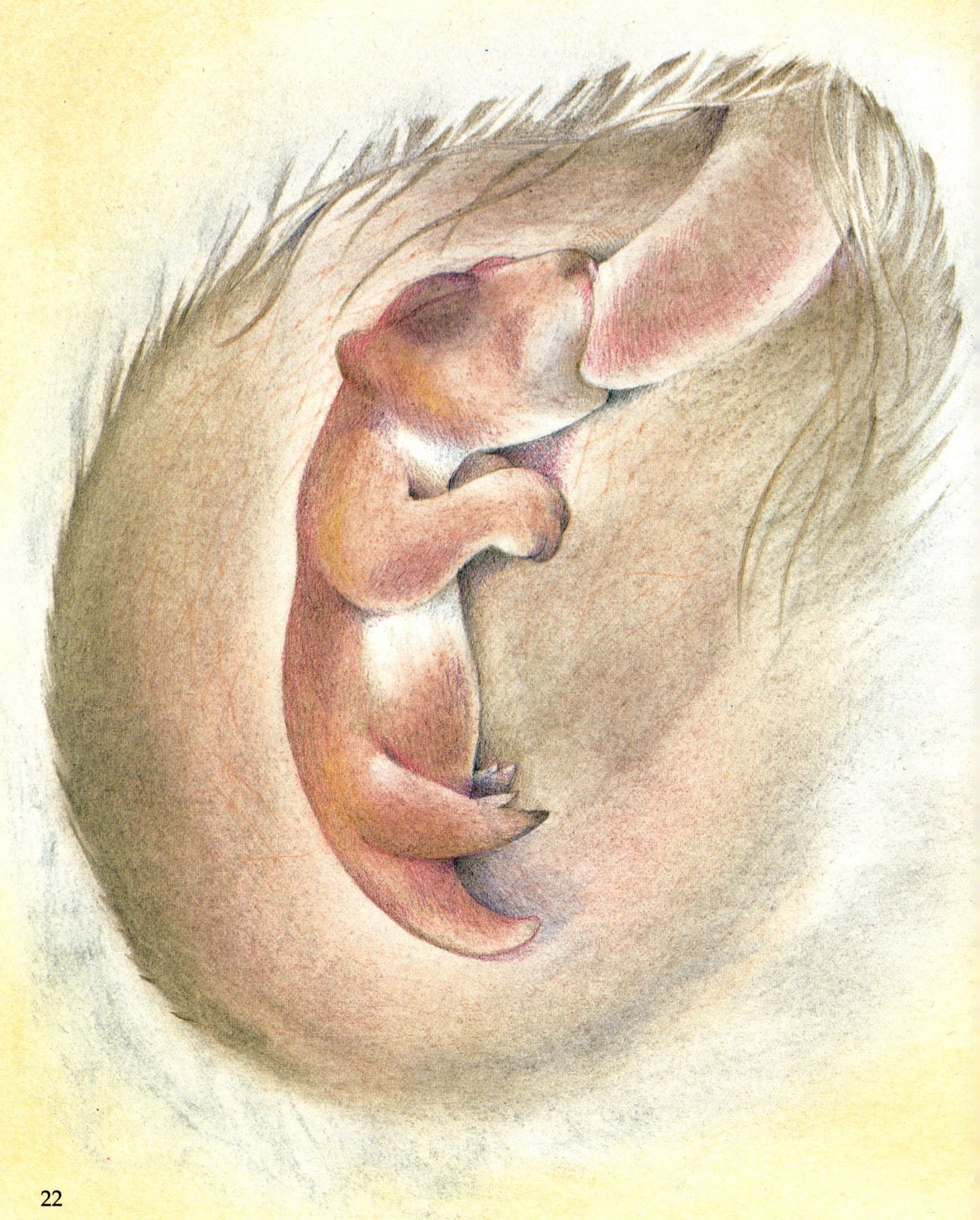

The tiny baby crawls into the pouch without help from its mother. For six months it stays inside and sucks milk.

As it gets older, the baby leaves the pouch each day. After eating and playing, it crawls back inside.

If large hungry lizards or snakes are near, the mother calls to her young. She makes soft clucking noises until the baby is safe.

At eight months the young kangaroo hops alongside its mother. Inside her pouch is another tiny baby.

wombat

Koalas, opossums, and wombats are like kangaroos. They carry their young in pouches. None grow as large or move as fast as the kangaroo.

GLOSSARY

These words are explained the way they are used in this book. Words of more than one syllable are in parentheses. The heavy type shows which syllables are stressed.

alongside (a·**long**·side) — close by
clucking (**cluck**·ing) — a sound like a click
defend (de·**fend**) — to protect against attack
dingo (**din**·go) — wild dog that hunts kangaroos
koala (ko·**a**·la) — a small, furry animal that lives in trees
lizard (**liz**·ard) — reptile with four legs and a long tail
mob — a group of kangaroos
newborn (**new**·born) — just born
opossum (o·**pos**·sum) — a small, furry animal, also called possum
pouch — part of a kangaroo's body that is like a bag
suck — to draw milk into the mouth
thump — a loud sound made when something is hit
water hole (**wa**·ter hole) — a small pond
wombat (**wom**·bat) — a furry animal that looks like a small bear